FEARLESS LIVING

FEARLESS LIVING

ARIC BLACKWOOD

CONTENTS

Introduction   1

1 Understanding Anxiety and Worry   3

2 Overcoming Fear and Embracing Courage   6

3 Strategies for Managing Anxiety   10

4 Building a Support System   14

5 Lifestyle Changes for Anxiety Relief   18

6 Facing and Conquering Specific Fears   21

7 Maintaining Long-Term Mental Well-being   24

Conclusion   27

Copyright © 2025 by Aric Blackwood
All rights reserved. No part of this book may be reproduced in any manner whatsoever without written permission except in the case of brief quotations embodied in critical articles and reviews.
First Printing, 2025

Introduction

The child's weeping ceased, his eyes widening in a mix of wonder and fear. "Please, Papa, doesn't it?" he gasped. The father, chuckling softly, shook his head and replied, "No, don't be silly." He enveloped the boy in a warm embrace, positioning him in such a way that both could now marvel at the spectacular display just above the rooftops. Greatly relieved, they both gazed at the magnificent scene. "Isn't it marvelous?" the father said, his voice filled with awe. "Doesn't it seem like such a grand show in the sky for someone so little?" The boy's tears vanished, his worry melting away. With his face glowing with newfound excitement, he asked, "Papa, won't the fairies feel cold?"

In this tender moment, a caring father helped his terrified five-year-old find security amidst the storm. The child had been frightened by the fierce lightning and thunder, bursting into a loud, sorrowful cry. His dad, ever the protector, scooped him up onto his lap, holding him tight and offering comfort. "Don't be afraid," he whispered reassuringly. "People aren't afraid of electricity. They welcome it into their homes and businesses, using it for cooking, lighting, heating, communication, and more. There's no need to be scared. Thunder doesn't expect anyone to be wimps. It takes the electricity out of the clouds and channels it down to the earth. Besides, our house has a sturdy lightning rod. It will protect us. We are safe."

The father continued, "Electricity is a powerful force, but it's also our ally. Imagine a world without it—so many of the things we take for granted would disappear. The lights that brighten our nights, the heat that warms us during winter, the devices that keep us connected—all rely on this incredible energy. Thunder and lightning are nature's way of reminding us of that power, but they're not to be feared. They are part of the same force that helps us every day. And with our lightning rod, we have an added layer of protection. It ensures that the electricity finds its way safely to the ground, keeping us out of harm's way."

The child, feeling the steady beat of his father's heart and the warmth of his embrace, began to see the storm in a new light. What once seemed like a monstrous, chaotic force was now a magnificent, awe-inspiring display of nature's grandeur. The fairies in the sky, imagined in his innocent mind, would be just fine, he thought. After all, if they could dance among the clouds and ride the bolts of lightning, surely they were used to a little cold.

CHAPTER 1

Understanding Anxiety and Worry

Anxiety and worry manifest themselves in distinctive ways across cognitive, emotional, and behavioral dimensions. Cognitively, they bring about confusion, preoccupation, impaired decision-making, difficulty concentrating, and challenges in logical thinking. Emotionally, they are marked by agitation, irritation, depression, a sense of helplessness, and feelings of numbness. Behaviorally, they can lead to rigidity, difficulties with work performance, impaired interpersonal relations, lack of motivation, and challenges in appraising emotions and emotional states. Additionally, anxiety and worry involve complex dynamics of positive and negative reinforcement. The degree to which each dimension of worry is experienced varies from individual to individual. A thorough understanding and assessment of these aspects is key to effective worry regulation.

Anxiety and worry can significantly impact one's quality of life. They can take over a person's existence, restricting their activities and, in severe cases, leading to panic attacks. To avoid potential danger, individuals may limit themselves to the confines of their fears. The focus of a fearful person's attention often narrows to thoughts about their inability to function normally, physical changes, and negative expectations. This can hinder proper communication, restrict the sharing of information, and limit an individual's potential.

Causes of Anxiety

Anxiety often arises when we are overly invested in the outcomes of situations. When we place excessive importance on an event and develop an unhealthy attachment to it, anxiety is triggered. Our assumptions about people or situations can distort our perceptions, leading to anxiety when reality doesn't align with our expectations. We become mortified when our rigid beliefs about someone or something don't fit the mold we've created, even subconsciously.

What drives people to experience the toxic emotion of anxiety? Many issues can be traced back to our over-attachment or clinging to something in life. Reflect on times when you have felt anxious. Whether it manifested physically with symptoms like a racing heart or by blowing a situation out of proportion (only to later recognize its futility), when does anxiety occur?

Effects of Anxiety on Mental Health

Anxiety serves as a constant reminder of our need to monitor our surroundings, often leading to increased levels of rapid-onset mental disorders, including Generalized Anxiety Disorder (GAD). GAD involves extreme or generalized fears, worries, or panic that significantly affect our overall well-being. It has surpassed major depressive disorder in its ability to create comorbidity within the general population. Among individuals suffering from GAD and major depression, 14.1% of adults aged 18-80 reported experiencing comorbid anxiety and depression symptoms in the past year. For those aged 60 and older, this rate jumped to about 27%.

The Covid-19 pandemic has brought anxiety to the forefront of mental health concerns. It has altered our thought processes, leading to a routine of focusing on worsening our current stressful situations. As the pandemic unfolded and the Center for Disease Control declared a pandemic, many people found themselves constantly checking news updates, believing that staying informed was essential to staying safe. The rapid increase in cases and documentation left many feeling overwhelmed by health warnings, zoning directives, and sensationalized accounts of the world, while our brains convinced us that our research was equipping us with the power to protect ourselves from the "invisible enemy."

Differentiating Anxiety and Worry

Our survival sense operates based on immediate feedback from present and apparently immediate future conditions. For example, an oncoming car seems to be moving toward you. It does not signal that a chair opposite you appears to be a large, menacing bear. Instead, it is our image-thinking and belief-system-based thinking that respond with fearful, anxious thoughts about potential dangers. When you are worrying or feeling anxious, you are not experiencing the immediate fear response of the moment; you are experiencing the belief-system fear panic that regards your confident self as a dumping ground for all the insecurity developed during identity formation.

The first step in freeing ourselves from fearful, worrisome thinking is to recognize that we cannot distinguish between anxiety and fear—thoughts produced by our survival fear response and our self-limiting, confidence-destroying worry. Our emotion system cannot differentiate between survival fear causing fearful thoughts and belief-system fear causing anxious thoughts. The fearfulness embedded in our belief system quickly triggers neural responses to fearful, insecurity-based scripting. This is why anxious thinking and panic attacks are so overwhelming and frustrating. These psychological emotional responses are instantaneous and powerful.

CHAPTER 2

Overcoming Fear and Embracing Courage

Fear is as old as life itself. Scientists suggest that fear is an ancient instinct, originating in our primitive past when humans lived in caves. What we fear can vary widely: for some, it is an obscure feeling, while for others, it is a clear and specific threat. Some associate their fear with isolated tragedies, while others are constantly haunted by the fear of the unknown and the incalculable, making it a permanent source of worry. We build our lives around fear, pain, and worry. When we reach old age, having exhausted much of our life, the fear of death often descends. This irony underscores the importance of striving for fearlessness. Can we achieve it? Yes, but it requires courage. Each of us has the capacity to carry our environment within ourselves, fostering non-dependence. A person is truly free when they are not subject to fear.

Fear is a product of our brain, and it is through sitting still and meditating that we can find solutions to the many problems created by fear and worries. For meditation to be effective, the environment must be conducive, allowing one to lead a normal daily life, generally unaffected by difficulties or tension. Joy can be found in life through self-discipline. The Upanishads liken the Atman (soul) to a bird sitting on a tree, observing the world without becoming entangled in it.

Fear does not discriminate; it affects the rich and poor, educated and illiterate alike. It suffocates joy and erases memories. Those who live their lives worrying about what the so-called "experts" say or do will never experience true joy. Fear immobilizes lives, replacing our work and daily activities with anxiety. Ultimately, fear and worry paralyze us, rendering us inert.

Identifying Fear Triggers

Urgent fears are instinctual responses, such as the fear of physical harm. Disgust is another urgent fear, triggered by the immediate threat of consuming something harmful, like rotten food. When faced with disgust, our survival instincts compel us to distance ourselves from the source. Urgent fears prompt action to maintain life. In contrast, anxiety lacks clear solutions and often requires facing the source rather than avoiding it. While fear can propel us to act quickly, anxiety lingers, requiring courage to confront.

Chronic fear can morph into generalized anxiety, making it difficult to pinpoint specific triggers. This generalized fear allows the brain's fear response reward system to continually produce dopamine. Living with non-specific fear can make it part of the background scenery of life. Over time, feelings of anxiety and despair become accepted as the norm. Urgent fears, while intense, are often easier to manage.

Developing a Growth Mindset

Dr. Carol Dweck of Stanford University distinguishes between a fixed mindset and a growth mindset. A fixed mindset assumes that abilities, intelligence, and talents are static, leading individuals to seek constant validation. In contrast, a growth mindset recognizes that talents and abilities can be developed through effort, good teaching, and persistence. This mindset helps individuals cope with anxiety and challenges more effectively, viewing life as a journey that requires time, work, and diligence.

Changing fearful beliefs doesn't require tackling each fear-producing thought directly. Embracing a growth mindset involves recognizing that intelligence and talents are not fixed traits but can be developed. This perspective fosters resilience and the ability to handle setbacks and obstacles without being crushed by failure.

Cultivating Self-Confidence

Self-confidence stems from understanding that we are part of something greater. Recognizing our skills and talents as gifts allows us to work diligently, knowing our role in life. Those who realize they are not the ultimate source of all good things approach their work with gratitude and dedication. They see their achievements as a result of collaboration with a higher power, focusing on learning and excelling in each task rather than seeking external validation.

High self-confidence individuals use their talents to help others and do good. They do not flaunt their abilities to make others feel inferior but instead work to uplift those around them. Gratitude and dedication to their work lead to a sense of fulfillment and a desire to continue improving.

Practicing Resilience

Resilience is a crucial skill that can be developed and enhanced at any stage of life. Research shows that moderate resilience, combined with protective factors like supportive relationships, a balanced diet, adequate rest, and physical, mental, and emotional stimulation, reduces the risk of emotional instability. Resilience is not built in the absence of problems but through managing and overcoming adversity. It involves learning to manage emotions and thoughts, particularly during highly adverse experiences.

In recent years, studies have demonstrated that resilience can be developed through practices like Worry Break-Up and Routine Release-Optional Relaxation®. These methods blend psychological flexibility with physiological release, helping individuals manage stress and build resilience. A small amount of worry and stress, known as eustress, can be beneficial, motivating us to overcome challenges like "writer's block" and fatigue.

CHAPTER 3

Strategies for Managing Anxiety

Anxiety might be a new experience for you, perhaps triggered by the birth of your first child. As each child arrives, new and different fears emerge—morning sickness, the baby's health, delivery, and daycare concerns. Anxiety could stem from recent changes in your health or that of a loved one. Old worry patterns might resurface with new intensity. Anxiety affects your personal identity and self-worth, often leading to doubt in your abilities as a parent, spouse, employee, or boss. Excessive worry can result in irritability, sadness, anger, and even depression. It creates internal chaos that is challenging to assess, control, and manage. Anxiety keeps us reacting, paralyzed, and even angry over hypothetical situations.

Understanding Anxiety

Anxiety is a normal part of life. No one is immune to anxious feelings, and we can't eliminate anxiety entirely. When you're anxious, you're essentially experiencing fear. Our brains react to perceived threats by increasing our heart rate and heightening our awareness. Emotionally, we feel "on edge" or expectant. While we might feel alone, it's important to remember that everyone experiences anxiety at times. Anxiety disorders are the most common mental health issues in the United States and likely in other countries. For some, anxiety leads to panic disorders, while others become consumed by worry that goes beyond what is normal and healthy. While a small amount of anxiety can help us focus or take action, excessive worry can constrict our lives to the point where we are barely living.

Deep Breathing Techniques

According to yogis, rhythmic, diaphragmatic, and conscientious breathing is the secret to life and youth, joy and exuberance, good health and longevity. Oxygen is the source of life. It purifies our bodies, enlivens us, empowers us with strength, and regenerates lost cells. It boosts memory, alleviates tension, and fulfills the mind. However, the daily grind and life's challenges make mindful breathing difficult. Living consciously and managing our intangible armory becomes almost impossible, and living with grace and splendor seems unattainable.

Breathing is the easiest and most effective relaxation, meditation, and visualization technique. When we breathe deeply and slowly through the diaphragm, the life force (prana) reaches our lungs, oozes through capillaries, enters the bloodstream, and invigorates every cell in our body. Conversely, shallow and rapid breathing allows fear to take hold. Since our breathing and thoughts are closely connected, managing our breathing is crucial for relaxation, de-stressing, meditating, or facing life challenges.

Mindfulness and Meditation

Just as you maintain your body, your brain needs careful attention. Self-discovery through mindfulness and occasional meditation provides mental jumpstarts. You'll start understanding the causes of your anxiety and minimize worries. You'll notice when you're making assumptions, carrying unnecessary stress, and dealing with worries that aren't yours. When overwhelmed by expectations, focus on the present and manage only what you can handle at the moment.

Reflect on decisions and reclaim your personal value when you give too little time to self-care. As your intentions, hopes, and assumptions become clearer, anxiety will lessen. You'll be more prepared to rely on internal trust and recognize your true value. While society may demand constant compensation, prioritize your own happiness. You are enough.

What you perceive is what you receive. If you dread making mistakes, you may inadvertently bring about what you fear. Be mindful of your thoughts and shift focus if you don't like what's dominating your consciousness. Meditation isn't about reaching specific states or changing your love of chocolate. It's about awareness, unity, peace, transforming thoughts, letting go, self-discovery, and mental cleansing. Dr. Jon Kabat-Zinn introduced mindfulness, transforming ancient Buddhist meditation practices into secular approaches for handling negative emotions and health problems. Mindfulness allows you to understand what's happening inside and around you.

Join millions who live in the present. Mindfulness means living right here, right now. Start your day with reflection and meditation, whether for a few minutes or longer. Meditation and mindful living help you get out of your head and into your body.

Cognitive-Behavioral Therapy

Cognitive-behavioral therapy (CBT) offers hope for those suffering from anxiety and depression. According to Albert Ellis, our thoughts shape our feelings. An irrational belief system can be identified and replaced with rational beliefs, reducing anxiety and depression. Ellis states, "Men are not disturbed by things but rather by their view of things." CBT theory suggests that changing your beliefs about a situation can change your emotional response. Just as faith in a higher power can provide peace, CBT offers a way to live free from anxiety.

From a biblical viewpoint, fear is rooted in unbelief. Jesus said, "Let not your heart be troubled, neither let it be afraid" (John 14:1). Trusting in God reduces symptoms of depression, anxiety, and fear. God wants us to experience security and peace in all situations, trusting Him regardless of our circumstances.

Physical Exercise and Relaxation

Learn to breathe slowly and relax your muscles. Various relaxation methods exist, such as tensing and releasing muscles. Take deep breaths to enhance relaxation. After twenty minutes of this practice, physical symptoms of anxiety will diminish, leaving you relaxed.

Regular exercise, even walking, helps regulate the body's chemical environment, reducing anxiety hormone production. Research shows that daily exercise lowers the likelihood of developing anxiety and panic attacks. If prone to anxiety, exercise can help you relax by reducing stress hormone production.

CHAPTER 4

Building a Support System

Initially, I was hesitant about joining a support group, but it turned out to be invaluable. Denise Onofrey, a psychotherapist from Ohio, emphasized the importance of having a support system in our lives. She highlighted how support systems promote and reinforce the value of connection and vulnerability. "Our culture has amplified fear and social isolation; many of us have grown up being shamed into thinking that our vulnerability was a sign of weakness." While society often emphasizes independence, I've discovered that there is strength in vulnerability. It requires others to witness it, and our support system strengthens us by being witnesses to our struggles, helping us realize that our vulnerability does not define us.

Vulnerability can be misconstrued as weakness, but I believe allowing someone to know you are struggling is an act of strength and humility. Overcoming anxiety or fear usually requires vulnerability, as it often involves hard work that we cannot do alone. We are not meant to go through life alone, especially when battling anxiety and worry. A strong support system can help us navigate our minds, and we need trustworthy people around us. This connection forces us to be vulnerable and authentic. Anxiety and worry are overwhelming enough without having to consider others' issues on top of our own.

Enlist friends who believe in you, will not judge, and understand your struggles. We need people who remind us that we are "loved and supported." Confiding in someone is one of the first steps, as it removes the isolating feeling of fighting alone. After confessing our struggles, friends can help us recognize patterns of worry and anxiety so we can change them. They can hold us accountable, especially if we revert to old patterns, and be proactive in covering our blind spots and helping when we are stressed.

Seeking Professional Help

The thought of seeking dedicated support for anxiety may be intimidating. For some, seeking help feels like admitting inadequacy. However, emotional suffering is just as real and dangerous as physical suffering. Yet, seeking care for emotional wounds rarely feels as permissible as seeking physical care. Healthcare is necessary for well-being, and seeking therapy and counseling is not a failure but a step toward well-being. Research shows many do not discuss emotional issues to remain strong or support others.

A life of fearless living begins with a conscious choice. Informed decision-making is required for sustainable living without worry. The art of fearless living draws from all human experiences to reduce symptoms of anxiety and eliminate worry. Professional help is often an essential part of acquiring health, success, and living well. While some may feel reluctant to use mental health services, guidance is necessary for maintaining balance and well-being. Professional guidance, including therapy and counseling, is a valuable resource for living fearlessly.

Connecting with Supportive Friends and Family

Fear may prompt you to seek comfort from others. Each time you reach out, you practice asking for and receiving help. Your willingness to share your fears is an opportunity to help others who are also afraid. Compassionate relationships connect and heal all involved. My best friend instantly calms me when I call her with worry, and she shares her worries with me. This strengthens our relationship and our ability to function productively.

Value the people who know how great you are. When anxiety or worry makes you feel uncertain, connect with friends and family who remind you that you are lovable, strong, and special. Catch a friend's eye, squeeze hands, laugh when you want to cry, and remember the good in yourself. These actions help pull you back to center and connect you to the strength that friends, family, and a good laugh can offer. Many therapists recommend building a social support network to address anxiety and stress. Helping someone through their worry and fear can also make you feel loved and strong when you seek support.

Joining Support Groups and Communities

Support groups can even be formed and operated by patients. Author Joan Dunphy's book "Hope in Hell: Inside the World of Doctors Without Borders" tells of a group of women on a psychiatric ward who organized their own treatment program. If forming your own group, Loveday and Wesselmann's book provides guidance. Support groups at mental health institutions are often organized and hosted by qualified workers, peers, nurses, or group leaders.

Support groups are an excellent form of treatment, meeting weekly at mental health institutions. Some are led by professionals and some by peers. They often become long-term, ongoing communities. Over the years, members come and go. Some are relieved of symptoms, while others may struggle. The goal is to help without professional intervention. Observe and understand these interactions. This type of treatment, though low-cost, can be the most impactful.

CHAPTER 5

Lifestyle Changes for Anxiety Relief

1. Eat Less Caffeine

If you struggle with anxiety, studies suggest significantly curtailing or eliminating caffeine from your diet. Caffeine can cause jitteriness and anxiety, especially when consumed in large doses or by sensitive individuals. It also seems to decrease the effectiveness of serotonin, a chemical produced in the brain and gut, and other neurotransmitters associated with reduced anxiety. For some people, stopping caffeine could turn anxiety into a passing pothole rather than a fixed state of mind. Additionally, consider increasing your intake of foods rich in the nutrients that help produce serotonin, dopamine, and norepinephrine at the right places and times in your brain.

2. Eat Less Sugar and Refined Carbs

Reducing sugar and refined carbs can break the anxiety cycle. When you consume refined carbs, your body quickly metabolizes them into sugar, leading to a spike in blood sugar levels. This spike is followed by a sharp drop, triggering your brain to search for more sugar. The result is a constant cycle of jitteriness and anxiety. By breaking this cycle, you can stabilize your body and mind chemistry.

Healthy Eating Habits

A diet education plan should aim to prevent the development of obesity and promote overall health. Within the family home, learning about healthy eating should be a daily act, integrated into routine situations. The emotional and cultural background of the family plays a significant role in this process. The internalization of societal rules is complex, and children remain subjective individuals within their social groups. Idealizing a pedagogical plan for the family should recognize socially accepted values, allowing the child's emotional and food management skills to develop based on familiar concepts.

Conversations about food within the family are crucial for emotional connections. Human strategies involve thinking about controlling reality before dealing with adverse situations. Dietary education should consider the management of emotions, as body and mind are part of a single complex system. Studies suggest that managing emotions through food education can help control other negative feelings.

Regular Sleep Patterns

Implementing regular sleep patterns is essential for well-being. Sleep renews us, and with it comes the confidence to let go of desperation, which often leads to anxiety. Without regular doses of peace and quiet, negative thinking patterns emerge. Deconstruct this cycle by making sleep a priority and using it as a sanctuary from the outside world. Peace of mind will be attracted to the safety that sleep brings, eventually nesting within us permanently.

Occasional sleepless nights are tolerable, but habitual sleeplessness spreads anxiety and fear. At night, our breath slows, and our minds and bodies become restful. Experiment with the following habits to improve sleep:

1. Turn off overhead lights.
2. Ignore the telephone.
3. Refrain from watching television.
4. Avoid using the computer. Embrace the natural relaxation of the night, and sleep will become a willing companion.

Stress Management Techniques

- Write out a daily schedule or to-do list. Checking things off your list can give you a sense of accomplishment.
- Set realistic goals and be gentle with yourself if you don't reach them.
- Make a list of tasks you can outsource to others. Whether hiring help or enlisting family members, delegating can lift a weight off your shoulders.

Spending time with pets is also a great way to manage stress. Here are additional tips for when you're feeling stressed:

- Avoid overscheduling yourself.
- Reduce caffeine and sugar intake.
- Practice portion control and regular exercise.
- Stick to a regular sleep schedule and avoid alcohol.
- Use aromatherapy and spend time in nature.
- Listen to music and maintain a daily routine.
- If possible, get regular massages for physical and emotional well-being.

CHAPTER 6

Facing and Conquering Specific Fears

In this book, I have created a life template composed of eight overarching principles and 15 strategies that put those principles into action. I call it Post-Dependence. While there are no guarantees that my plan will work for everyone, it offers a roadmap for gradually releasing yourself from fear. Each person's journey is unique, and even if you follow my plan, you will still be you in the end. You are an extraordinary person with unique potential. When you live to your potential, your possibilities are not ordinary but dazzling. Ultimately, it is up to you to take this journey. Post-Dependence is a roadmap to explore what is possible, and I hope the map and accompanying stories inspire you to embark on the bold adventures you deserve.

In recent years, I have received countless inquiries from people who believe anxiety and worry are holding them back. They struggle to understand why they feel this way and often label themselves as "broken" or "odd." Some have found partial success in healing, while others have made little progress. Is it possible that deep-seated fear is behind your anxiety and worry? Could an unidentified or ingrained response to fear be causing your struggle with peace and progress?

Public Speaking Anxiety

Public speaking anxiety is a common fear. My family members weren't thrilled about public speaking either, but they didn't see it as a reason to avoid educational endeavors. My intense fear of public speaking seemed ridiculous to everyone but me. Their advice and suggestions felt like misguided fortune-telling. My fear was so great that even fake conversations on the radio made me woozy, sweaty, and delusional.

I would have driven sixty miles for a phone call. My fear of public speaking was that intense. With rubbery legs, perspiration blooming like mushrooms, and vocal cords crushed into a pulpy mass of nerves, I was tormented by anxiety. I relied on visual conversations on paper and wrote thousands of notes to my sons. After a tragic car accident, my fear became so intense that making appointments for myself or my boys felt like an insurmountable task.

Social Anxiety

Social anxiety is rooted in the perception that others are potentially hostile. It extends from the constant fear of wounding, mistreatment, or abuse, whether real or imagined. This sensitivity stems from the frustration of essential social needs for acceptance, approval, appreciation, and love. Without these social needs, children cannot survive. As we grow, our value systems expand through experience, and the source of perpetual anxiety becomes clear—we fear not being our ideal selves or failing to meet expectations.

Fear arises when we imagine others judging us and finding us wanting. We dread embarrassment, but who are these people? Can we trust their judgments? Often, the harshest critic in our minds is someone who hasn't done meaningful work on the topic. Mastery of living and excelling in any area is yours. Apply 100% interest in your successes and 100% judgment in your assessments.

Fear of Failure

Fear of failure often manifests as a desire to remain inconspicuous. This fear is one of the most common, even more than illness or death. Behind the fear of public speaking, for example, there may be numerous other fears. A teacher feared teaching mathematics if students used both hands, stemming from various events. Exploring our past can be painful, and sometimes it is more challenging than facing the present.

Fear of failure can lead to defiant refusals. For instance, a patient refusing a simple task like hanging clothes may cite a fear of failure. This fear often involves a wish to avoid shame, rejection, or vulnerability. Failure becomes a means of self-protection against perceived inadequacy.

CHAPTER 7

Maintaining Long-Term Mental Well-being

These demands and limitations actually bring freedom. I strive to live boldly, exercising courage. My efforts, supported by grace, enhance my divine greatness, allowing me to live a joyful, fearless life filled with satisfaction, tranquility, and discipline. By living in reason and virtue, I elevate myself, not through imaginary devices, but by the energy of my soul and spirit. Techniques for achieving tranquility come through divine inspiration, flooding and permeating my being. We learn to discipline our minds, not by focusing on material outcomes, but by relinquishing desires and pursuing tranquility.

We often worry, fear, and ruminate on negative thoughts, memories, and sensations. This process is maintained by our continued attention to these imaginative products. By disciplining our minds and ignoring the urge to seek pleasure and avoid pain, we take the first step in mental training, helping to rid ourselves of worry and ambition. Ancient wisdom tells us to live in reason, practicing discipline and fortitude. By practicing mental suppleness, restraint, and justice, we become resilient. Pain diminishes because we train ourselves in this activity, making it a habit. Just as runners endure discipline to run safely, we must learn mental discipline to live freely.

Self-Care Practices

Implementing effective self-care practices can enhance emotional and physical health. Here are some beneficial practices: get enough sleep, eat nutritious foods, drink more water, take walks, exercise daily, establish a workout routine, make time for hobbies, socialize, show affection, take breaks from the news, avoid toxic people, find a new therapist if needed, and practice daily relaxation exercises. Remember, if you don't make time for self-care, you'll be forced to make time for illness.

Self-care involves deliberate activities to take care of mental, emotional, and physical health. Although simple in theory, it is often overlooked. Good self-care improves mood, reduces anxiety, and fosters good relationships. It's essential for feeling better about ourselves and our abilities. Self-care also means acknowledging when you need a break and giving yourself that break. Sometimes, self-care can feel like a chore, but ignoring it will only worsen worry and stress, affecting both mental and physical health.

Setting Realistic Goals

Realistically, not everyone will recognize your anxiety. Others have their own concerns and generally don't want to draw attention to your distress. Realizing this can help calm some symptoms. If you acknowledge your anxiety and leave the room, it makes the task more difficult next time. Acting on your intentions despite your feelings can lead to progress. Facing feared situations incrementally helps leave anxiety and panic in the past.

Consider the scenario of an anxious woman entering a room full of strangers. Her thoughts race, her heart pounds, and she panics about her panic. Her body shakes, her palms are clammy, and her tongue dries up. The simple act of walking becomes overwhelming.

In such moments, it's crucial to recognize that most people are not focused on her, and facing the situation can help reduce anxiety over time.

Celebrating Achievements

Apply what you've learned to achieve harmony and balance in your life. When fear creeps in, center yourself with quiet stillness. Embrace the power of the moment with patience and grace. Other ways to reduce fear include aligning with religious or spiritual beliefs, savoring the joy of others, finding your purpose, accepting life's uncertainties, and celebrating gratitude. Accepting the paradox that suffering creates joy can replace anxiety with balance, joy, and happiness. Chemical changes will reduce stress, restore our immune systems, and reestablish biological equilibrium. Practicing moments of quietness, regardless of circumstances, is key to reducing fear.

Now is a good time to identify and affirm your achievements in conquering fear. Write down your answers to the following questions:

- What have I achieved?
- How did I face my fears?
- What progress have I made?

Remember, your bravery lies not in flawless achievement but in persistence. Each time you faced your fear, you moved closer to a life of increased faith, courage, health, and fulfillment. Celebrate your hard-earned calm and feel proud of your work. Fear is like a river—you must release your grip to flow joyously and find strength.

Conclusion

Reflecting on my journey, I initially thought that some parts of this process seemed haphazard, as if trying to cover too much. I was wrong. The essence of the original concepts has been recapped here with more detail and practical ways of implementing those principles, full of countless thought-provoking exercises. This alone has made it more than worth the effort. The exercises, while abundant, are just part of it. Understanding and putting into practice the AOP process—Acceptance, Observation, Proclamation—was invaluable.

My personal favorite is the AOP process. At first, it required continuous mental discipline, but it gradually became a habit, a natural way of thinking. Fear has much less of a hold on me and my life now. If you appreciate the 12-step program and want to embark on a path to fearless living, I highly recommend this approach. In my opinion, as far as practical self-help books go, Susan Jeffers came closest to saying it all.

I was initially concerned that without having read Susan Jeffers' first book, *Feel the Fear and Do It Anyway*, I might be at a disadvantage. This book did have a kind of 'sequel' feel to it. After reading *Feel the Fear and Do It Anyway*, I explored other books recommended by Jeffers, such as *Feeling Fear* (about dealing with long-term illness) and *Embracing Uncertainty*, as well as her book on relationships. Then I found *Fearless Living*. It turned out to be a 'sequel' to Jeffers' bestseller, and a step-by-step practical guide to implementing the philosophy outlined in the previous volume by gradually eliminating old thought patterns and adopting a new attitude.

I already had several steps installed, but *Fearless Living* presents everything clearly, with each of the 12-15 mechanisms having its proper place in the whole. I made it my guidebook over the winter, and it's been gratifying to see a noticeable change. Of course, there's a long way ahead, but unlike in the past, I now feel confident that I can make it. I enjoy the process and maintain my optimism and enthusiasm, even when I encounter obstacles.

This book has been a transformative journey, offering practical exercises, insightful strategies, and a new way of thinking. By embracing the principles and practices outlined here, I have found a path to fearless living, filled with increased faith, courage, health, and fulfillment.

www.ingramcontent.com/pod-product-compliance
Lightning Source LLC
LaVergne TN
LVHW092102060526
838201LV00047B/1533